SPACE DISCOVERY GUIDES

GARBAGE IN SPACE

A SPACE DISCOVERY GUIDE

Margaret J. Goldstein

Lerner Publications ◆ Minneapolis

Lerner Publications Company
A division of Lerner Publishing Group, Inc.
241 First Avenue North
Minneapolis, MN 55401 USA

For reading levels and more information, look up this title at www.lernerbooks.com.

Main body text set in Avenir LT Std 65 Medium 11.5/17.5.
Typeface provided by Adobe Systems.

Library of Congress Cataloging-in-Publication Data

Names: Goldstein, Margaret J.
Title: Garbage in space: a space discovery guide/ Margaret J. Goldstein.
Description: Minneapolis : Lerner Publications, [2017] | Series: Space discovery guides | Audience: Age 9–12. | Audience: Grade 4 to 6. | Includes bibliographical references and index.
Identifiers: LCCN 2016018175 (print) | LCCN 2016021943 (ebook) | ISBN 9781512425901 (lb : alk. paper) | ISBN 9781512427981 (eb pdf)
Subjects: LCSH: Space debris—Juvenile literature. | Space pollution—Juvenile literature.
Classification: LCC TL1499 .G65 2017 (print) | LCC TL1499 (ebook) | 2 - 44493 - 23302 - 3/14/2018

LC record available at https://lccn.loc.gov/2016018175

Manufactured in the United States of America
1-41358-23302-4/21/2016

TABLE OF CONTENTS

A group of Vietnamese officials inspect a metal container believed to be a Russian air tank that fell from space.

In January 2016, a sound like thunder rumbled through the skies of northern Vietnam. Right after that, three round, metal containers fell to the ground. The largest container, about 39 inches (99 centimeters) across and about 99 pounds (45 kilograms), came to rest near a stream. A smaller container landed in a neighborhood yard. The smallest one hit a roof and then rolled onto the ground.

Officials from Vietnam's defense department examined the containers. The investigation showed that they were tanks for holding compressed air and that they'd been made in Russia. One aerospace expert guessed that the tanks had come from an artificial satellite, a human-made craft designed to orbit (circle around) Earth in space.

Controlled by humans on the ground, more than a thousand working satellites orbit Earth. They do different jobs, such as studying weather, transmitting telephone signals, and making photographs of Earth from space. Most people rarely think about satellites. But occasionally parts of satellites and other spacecraft come crashing to the ground, reminding us that the space around Earth is not empty. Not only is it home to satellites, it is also home to millions of pieces of human-made debris, commonly called space junk.

Sometimes old satellites explode, shooting pieces of debris into space.

This large piece of space junk landed in Texas after falling from orbit.

DANGER ZONE

This wasn't the first time something had fallen to Earth from space. Space junk has been a growing problem ever since space exploration began. In 2013, for example, about 600 pounds (272 kg) of metal from a European satellite fell from the sky and landed in the South Atlantic Ocean. And this kind of garbage is even more dangerous in space. Millions of pieces of metal, old spacecraft, and satellites orbit Earth at up to 17,500 miles (28,164 kilometers) per hour. Working spacecraft and astronauts have a high chance of being hit by this orbiting garbage. In fact, in 2015, three astronauts aboard the International Space Station (ISS) were ready to head back to Earth in a space capsule to avoid being hit by a piece of a satellite hurtling toward them.

The space around Earth is filled with so much junk that agencies on the ground monitor it around the clock. They track all but the smallest pieces of space junk using radar, telescopes, and other equipment. If monitors see that a large piece of junk is headed for a spacecraft or a satellite, they alert the craft's controllers, who move the craft out of the way.

Orbiting space junk made this hole in a satellite (*inset*). Operators in the main control room for the European Space Agency (ESA) monitor space junk and control spacecraft (*below*).

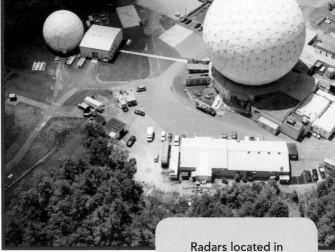

This telescope, in Spain, searches for asteroids and tracks the orbits of objects in space (*above*).

Radars located in Massachusetts collect data about garbage in space for NASA.

But as the amount of junk in space grows, it might become impossible for spacecraft to avoid it. George Zamka was an astronaut with the National Aeronautics and Space Administration (NASA), the US agency in charge of spaceflight. He said in 2014 that "during my two space missions, we flew upside down and backwards [in a space shuttle] to protect our shuttle windows from orbital debris. And even doing that, we had debris strikes and cracks in our windows."

Space experts say that humans need to clean up the junk in space before it damages more spacecraft. They say that if we don't get the space junk problem under control, it might become impossible for astronauts to safely leave the planet to explore our solar system.

NASA is developing a radar system to better track objects in Earth's orbit (*above*). NASA laser expert Barry Coyle works to develop a laser device for tracking garbage in space (*left*).

These images show how space junk has increased over the years.

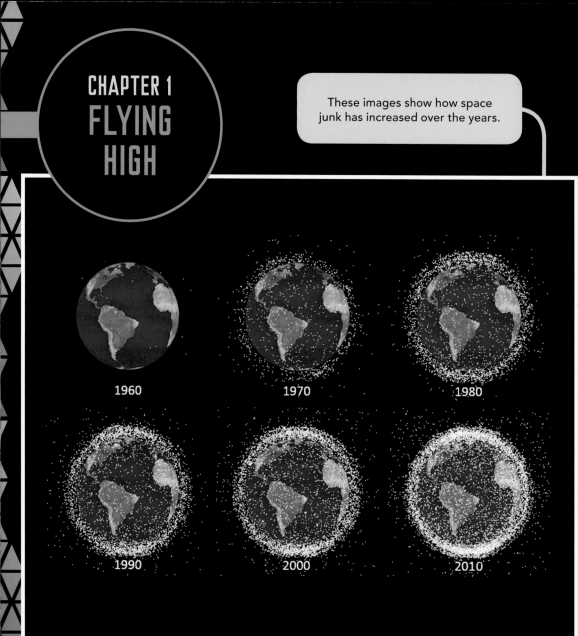

1960

1970

1980

1990

2000

2010

In the 1950s, when humans first began exploring space, no one worried about space junk. After all, the space around Earth is vast. With the exception of natural objects such as asteroids and meteors (flying chunks of metal and rock), the space was completely empty before human spaceflight.

The Soviet Union (a nation that existed from 1922 to 1991, based in modern-day Russia) launched the world's first spacecraft into orbit in 1957. The United States quickly followed with its own spacecraft in 1958. In 1960 the United States launched *Echo I*, NASA's first communications satellite.

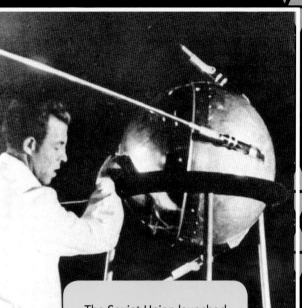

The Soviet Union launched *Sputnik 1*, the first spacecraft, in 1957.

People quickly realized the value of satellites. Research satellites can collect information about Earth, space, and the solar system. Weather satellites can gather data on atmospheric conditions and help make weather forecasts.

NASA's first communications satellite, *Echo I*, was launched in 1960.

Communications satellites can relay radio, TV, and telephone signals. Navigational satellites can help airplanes, ships, and other vehicles determine their locations on Earth. Military satellites allow governments to monitor the activities of enemy nations. In the late twentieth century, governments and businesses around the world launched more than one hundred satellites each year.

TRAFFIC JAM

Space became more and more crowded. The United States and the Soviet Union built several space stations, or orbiting research laboratories for astronauts. The United States also built a fleet

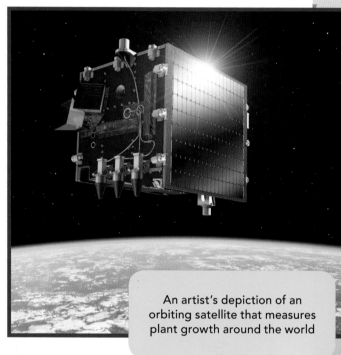

An artist's depiction of an orbiting satellite that measures plant growth around the world

of space shuttles, vehicles that were carried into space by rockets but landed on their own like airplanes. By the late twentieth century, the once vast emptiness of space around Earth was filled with satellites, spacecraft, and other vehicles.

Along with space vehicles came space junk. When satellites ran out of fuel or broke down, operators on the ground usually left them to drift in space. Astronauts on space walks (working outside their spacecraft) sometimes dropped tools, nuts and bolts, cameras, and other gear by accident, adding more junk

to the mix. Sometimes broken-down satellites and other vehicles exploded or crashed into one another. The fragments from the explosions and collisions became more space junk. Space junk even ended up on the moon. Astronauts traveling there in the late 1960s and early 1970s brought landing craft, rovers, cameras, food containers, and other gear. When the astronauts left the moon, much of the junk stayed behind.

Astronauts on space walks may create space junk by dropping tools or equipment.

An artist's depiction shows a spacecraft burning up as it enters Earth's atmosphere.

WHAT GOES UP MUST COME DOWN

Satellites and orbiting spacecraft travel at high speeds. Rockets launch them into orbit at about 17,500 miles (28,164 km) per hour. Space vehicles must move this fast to counter the force of gravity. If they were to slow down, gravity would eventually pull them back to Earth.

Once a vehicle or piece of space junk is orbiting at high speed, it will continue to speed through space for years or even decades. Even satellites that have burned up all their fuel and lost communications with humans on the ground (known as zombie satellites) will continue to travel at 17,000-plus miles (27,359 km) per hour.

Eventually, gravity pulls zombies and other pieces of space junk back to the atmosphere, but this takes a long time. The time frame depends on how close the objects are to Earth. Objects more than 620 miles (998 km) above Earth will continue to orbit for one hundred years or more before falling. Objects about 500 miles (805 km) above Earth will fall within decades. The closest objects, orbiting 370 miles (595 km) above Earth or lower, will fall in just a few years.

Scientists report that about two or three pieces of space junk fall into Earth's atmosphere every day. That adds up to about 100 to 150 tons (91 to 136 metric tons) of space junk per year. As they fall, pieces of junk rub against gases in the air, grow extremely hot, break apart, and burn up. During the daytime, with the sun lighting up the sky, you're unlikely to see this fiery junk. But people often report seeing bright lights streaking through the dark sky at night. Some of these streaks are meteors. Others are burning pieces of space junk.

A Japanese spacecraft breaks up after reentering Earth's atmosphere over Australia.

A US customs officer inspects the largest piece of Skylab after it landed in Australia.

Sometimes pieces of debris, such as the air tanks that fell in Vietnam in 2016, don't burn up completely. They fall to the ground or land in the ocean. The most famous case of plummeting space junk occurred in 1979 when Skylab, a US space station, fell from its orbit. Much of the station burned up high in the atmosphere, but some large pieces landed in Western Australia. No one was hit or hurt by the falling debris.

US Federal Emergency Management Agency workers inspect damage caused by a piece of the *Columbia* space shuttle.

In a tragic accident in 2003, the space shuttle *Columbia* broke apart and burned up during reentry. All seven astronauts aboard were killed, and small pieces of debris from the shuttle fell to the ground across Texas. In the fall of 2013, an ESA satellite ran out of fuel and fell from its orbit. Most of the satellite burned up high in the atmosphere. But some parts of the craft didn't burn completely. The ESA reported that several dozen pieces of the satellite—totaling about 600 pounds (272 kg) of metal and other material—landed in the South Atlantic Ocean between Antarctica and South America.

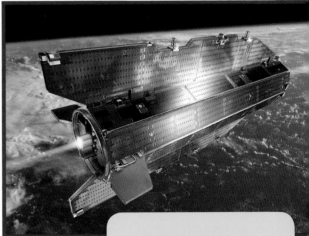

This artist's depiction shows an ESA satellite in orbit.

CHAPTER 2
THE
JUNKYARD

These red and green lines show the spread of debris one year after two satellites collided in orbit.

On February 10, 2009, a zombie Russian satellite, *Cosmos 2251,* crashed into an operating US communications satellite, *Iridium 33.* The crash caused trouble on the ground. It briefly disrupted telephone service for some customers of the Iridium communications company. But the damage in space was far more severe. *Cosmos* and *Iridium,* each traveling at about 17,500 miles (28,164 km) per hour, slammed into each other and blasted apart into thousands of fragments of metal, glass, paint, and plastic.

These fragments joined a growing body of junk already orbiting Earth in space. According to NASA, Earth's orbit contains about five hundred thousand pieces of space junk the size of a marble or larger. That number includes about twenty-six hundred zombie satellites. NASA estimates that millions of smaller pieces of junk are also traveling through Earth's orbit.

An illustration shows the spread of debris from *Iridium 33* and *Cosmos 2251* twenty minutes after they collided.

THE KESSLER SYNDROME

US astrophysicist Donald Kessler first identified the space junk problem in the late 1970s. He explained how space junk creates more space junk. When a large piece of junk hits something in space, it breaks up into smaller pieces. With more pieces of junk flying through space, the potential for strikes increases. And more strikes create more space junk.

Donald Kessler

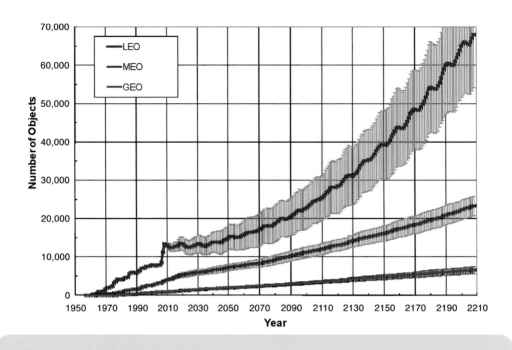

This graph shows the amount of space junk expected in low-earth orbit (LEO), mid-Earth orbit (MEO), and geostationary orbit (GEO, a type of high-earth orbit) over the years.

In 2013 Kessler said that space junk was multiplying faster than the force of gravity was pulling junk back into the atmosphere to burn up. Scientists named this process the Kessler Syndrome.

Kessler said that even if humans stopped launching new spacecraft, the amount of space junk would continue to grow. But businesses and governments do keep launching new spacecraft. From 2014 to 2023, an estimated 115 new satellites would go into space every year. The newest trend in satellites involves SmallSats, or satellites weighing less than 1,100 pounds (500 kg). Some of them are tiny: they weigh just a few ounces and can fit in a person's hand. These satellites operate similarly to larger satellites, but they are less expensive and easier to make. More and more private businesses are launching these tiny satellites, which only add to the growing space junk problem.

The Cooperative Research Centre for Space Environment Management in Australia

Avoiding Disaster

Researchers in Australia say that space junk threatens not only space exploration but also modern life and economy. In 2014 the Cooperative Research Centre (CRC) for Space Environment Management near Canberra, Australia, was established to address the issue.

"We depend on satellites to run just about everything in our society," CRC chief executive officer Ben Greene said. Greene believes that if space junk is not taken care of, satellites will continue to collide and that they could eventually all be destroyed. This would cause humans to lose everything from weather information to cell phone signals. The CRC is working to develop ways to track and eliminate more than three hundred thousand pieces of garbage in space. The CRC hopes to use lasers (devices that produce powerful beams of light) to quickly direct space junk toward Earth's atmosphere to burn up.

On top of this, humans continue to launch space capsules and other craft. All this space traffic, combined with the junk and working spacecraft already in orbit, will only make the space junk problem worse. In 2011 a general with the US Air Force Space Command predicted that space junk numbers could triple by the year 2030.

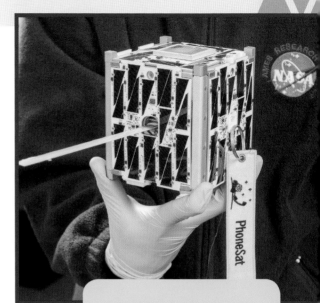

A NASA Smartphone satellite ready for launch in 2014

▶ HITS AND MISSES

The ISS travels in a junk-heavy zone called low-Earth orbit (112 to 1,243 miles, or 180 to 2,000 km, above Earth). Guided by trackers on the ground, the station frequently changes course to avoid oncoming junk. In July 2015, trackers detected a piece of junk from an old Russian weather satellite speeding toward the ISS.

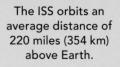

The ISS orbits an average distance of 220 miles (354 km) above Earth.

Screens in the ISS Mission Control room help monitor various systems aboard the space station (*above*). Flight director Courtenay McMillan monitors a spacecraft from the Mission Control Center (*inset*).

There was no time to maneuver the station out of harm's way. So the three astronauts aboard the ISS scrambled into a space capsule docked at the station. They remained there for about ten minutes, waiting to see if the junk was going to hit. If that seemed likely, the astronauts would have escaped in the capsule and hurried back to Earth. As it turned out, the junk sailed wide of the station, and the astronauts resumed their work on the ISS.

Astronauts on space walks are extremely vulnerable to space junk hits. Outside their craft, astronauts wear multilayer space suits, containing the same kinds of fabrics found in bulletproof vests. If a tiny, dust-sized piece of junk hits a space suit, it won't pierce the fabric. But a larger piece of junk, such as a nut or bolt from a zombie spacecraft, could puncture a space suit and kill the astronaut. So, in September 2009, ISS mission controllers watched cautiously as a piece of junk from an old European rocket zoomed toward the station. Two astronauts were scheduled for a space walk later that week.

Astronaut Michael Good makes repairs to the Hubble Space Telescope (*top*). Astronauts on space walks are in danger of being hit by space junk (*bottom*).

The Hubble Space Telescope connected to the *Atlantis* space shuttle during repairs to the telescope in 2009.

Controllers considered delaying it. As it turned out, the piece of junk traveled past the station at a distance of 2 miles (3.2 km). The space walk continued as planned. Also in 2009, before astronauts made a space walk to repair the Hubble Space Telescope, NASA engineers crunched some numbers. Their calculations revealed that the astronauts risked a 1 in 221 chance of getting hit by junk when they were making their repairs. Despite the risk, the astronauts safely completed their job.

CHAPTER 3
COPING WITH SPACE JUNK

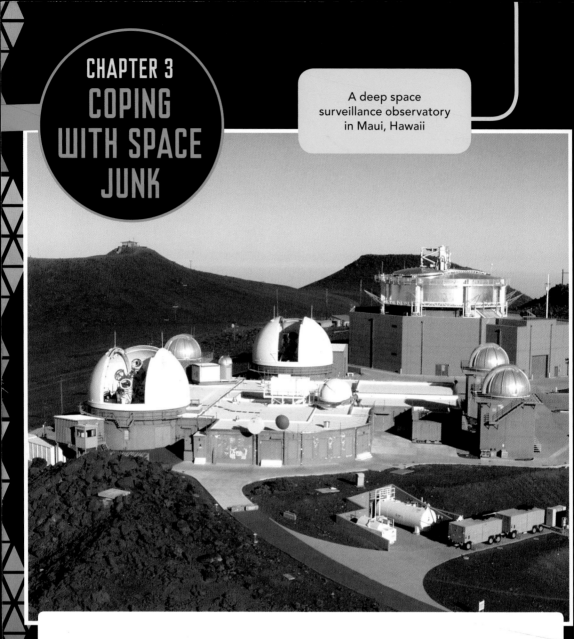

A deep space surveillance observatory in Maui, Hawaii

Space and military agencies around the world detect and track space junk using many tools. They gather data with telescopes, radar, and optical sensors on the ground. Satellites and space telescopes orbiting Earth also track junk and send data to trackers on the ground. Tracking agencies from different nations share information with one another to prevent space junk strikes.

In the United States, the US Department of Defense (DOD) operates the Space Surveillance Network. Its tracking equipment can detect objects in low-Earth orbit as small as 2 inches (5 cm) across. But more distant objects are harder to find. To spot them, DOD trackers have a new telescope, which was set up in Western Australia in 2016. Called the Space Surveillance Telescope, this powerful instrument can quickly scan the skies for small and dark objects. It can see into a faraway zone called high-Earth orbit, more than 22,000 miles (35,406 km) above the planet.

The unique lens design of the Space Surveillance Telescope allows it to see small objects in space.

The Space Surveillance Telescope dome in Western Australia was set up in 2016.

The telescope will help trackers find smaller and more distant objects than could be seen in the past.

Using their various tools, trackers on Earth carefully watch debris and note when a specific piece is headed toward a satellite, the ISS, or another craft. When they receive warning of an impending space junk strike, mission controllers and satellite operators reroute vehicles to avoid the oncoming junk.

ARMORED CARS

By 2016 US and Russian agencies were tracking more than twenty-three thousand pieces of junk. Tracking has its limits, however. Many pieces of debris are too small to track. And sometimes junk moves so quickly that spacecraft don't have time to move out of its way, even with advanced warning. Most craft end up with pits and dents made by tiny pieces of junk traveling at lightning speeds. For instance, in 2007 a piece of junk pierced a radiator panel on the US space shuttle *Endeavour*. In 2013 another fragment punched a hole through a solar panel on the International Space Station. The damaged parts of the spacecraft had to be repaired.

Because space junk strikes are unavoidable, all space vehicles are equipped on the outside with thick multilayer

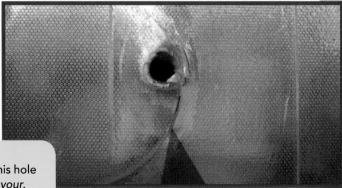

A piece of debris punched this hole in the space shuttle *Endeavour*.

One of the solar panels on the ISS was damaged by space junk in 2013 (*above*). All spacecraft have layered shields to stop space junk from damaging the craft (*right*).

shields. Made of bulletproof fabrics sandwiched between aluminum plates, the shields are designed to stop space junk.

When a piece of junk smashes into the outer, aluminum layer of a shield, it usually makes a dent and breaks up into a cloud of debris. But sometimes space junk pierces the outer layer. When this happens, the inner layers of fabric slow and stop the object. This system keeps space junk from damaging important instruments and equipment inside vehicles.

Shields can do a good job protecting spacecraft, but engineers note that after many space junk hits, shields can weaken. They might need to be repaired or replaced. Scientists at the Planetary and Space Science Centre at the University of New Brunswick in Canada are testing new, stronger materials that might be used to make improved spacecraft shields. The scientists even want to develop "self-healing" shields that can repair themselves after a space junk strike.

DAMAGE CONTROL

The more scientists can learn about space junk, the better they can protect vehicles in space. Certain spacecraft, such as astronaut capsules and some satellites, are designed to return to Earth intact.

Some spacecraft are covered by heat shields to keep them from burning up in Earth's atmosphere.

An example of the imaging equipment Lockheed Martin uses to track garbage in space

Eyes on the Sky

The Lockheed Martin aerospace company and the US Air Force are developing a new system to track smaller pieces of space junk than ever before. The new system, called the Space Fence, will detect and track objects as small as 1 inch (2.5 cm) across. It will also scan far more of the space around Earth than existing tracking systems. This means it will detect more junk. Whereas existing systems track about twenty-three thousand objects, the Space Fence is expected to track about two hundred thousand. The Space Fence will use radar and lasers to locate small pieces of space junk. It is expected to go online in 2018.

They are covered with heat shields that keep them from burning up on reentry. When these vehicles come back to Earth, aerospace engineers study the pits and dents caused by space junk. By looking at the size and number of dents, engineers can estimate how many tiny pieces of untrackable junk are traveling through space.

Scientists are also studying space junk itself. In one test in April 2014, NASA deliberately destroyed a full-size mock satellite inside a foam-lined chamber. The mock satellite had the same kinds of solar panels, antennae, computers, and other equipment one finds on a real working satellite. The researchers shot a 1.2-pound (0.5 kg) missile at the mock satellite at a speed of more than 15,000 miles (24,140 km) per hour. The satellite

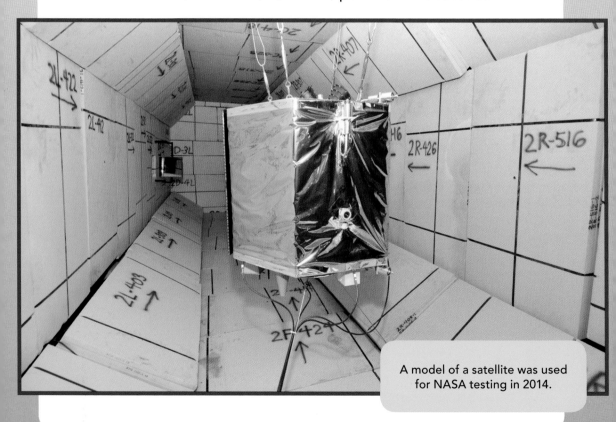

A model of a satellite was used for NASA testing in 2014.

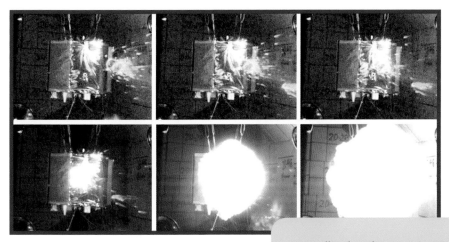

A satellite breaks apart in a NASA test, helping researchers understand what happens during a space junk strike.

broke apart into about eighty-five thousand pieces. Researchers then studied and measured the pieces. The test gave engineers an understanding of how materials used in satellites, such as metal, plastics, and carbon fibers, break apart during a space junk strike. The information will help engineers design new satellites that can better survive a strike.

CHAPTER 4
CLEANING
HOUSE

This artist's image shows the number of objects orbiting Earth at various distances.

When a satellite reaches the end of its life, operators on the ground have several options. The first is to simply let the satellite drift in orbit as a zombie. That's what satellite operators did throughout most of the years of human space travel.

An artist's depiction shows a zombie satellite that scientists lost contact with in 2012.

GRAVEYARD SHIFT

Another option is to steer the satellite, before it runs out of fuel, into a high orbit known as the geostationary graveyard. The graveyard is 22,400 miles (36,049 km) above Earth and about 200 miles (322 km) above even the highest-orbiting operational satellites. At this height, a zombie is unlikely to strike a working satellite. Many satellite operators use the graveyard option, but it is not an ideal fix. Even the geostationary graveyard is becoming crowded with zombies. And it might take one hundred years or more, but zombies will eventually fall from the graveyard. They could collide with operational satellites on the way down.

An illustration of an object entering Earth's atmosphere

This satellite image shows a part of the South Pacific Ocean known as the spacecraft cemetery.

Yet another option is to direct satellites, right before they are out of fuel, broken down, or finished with their missions, back into the atmosphere. Small satellites will burn up and disintegrate high in the air as they fall. However, big satellites and large vehicles such as space stations might not burn up completely. No one wants big chunks of metal striking the ground, as happened when Skylab fell in 1979. So mission controllers sometimes use another approach. They direct falling satellites and spacecraft to a remote part of the South Pacific Ocean. The craft mostly burn up high in the atmosphere, but any portions that don't burn land in the water. They sink into a deep undersea trench called the spacecraft cemetery. The cemetery holds the remains of more than 160 space vehicles. Large sections of Mir, an old Soviet/Russian space station, rest in the cemetery. When space agencies decide to shut down the ISS, which will likely happen in the 2020s, they might direct its remains to the spacecraft cemetery.

▶ REUSE, REFUEL, AND RECYCLE

When a satellite breaks down or runs out of fuel, operators on the ground usually send up a replacement. The new satellite takes over for the old one, whether the job is collecting data about Earth's atmosphere, making photographs of Earth, sending communications signals, or doing something else. The new satellite goes up, but the old one doesn't necessarily come down.

A better option would be to repair or refuel old satellites rather than cluttering up space with new ones. In previous years, this fix wasn't realistic. In a few cases, NASA sent astronauts in space shuttles to repair satellites. But such repairs were not the norm. Usually, broken satellites were simply replaced.

Sending astronauts into space to repair satellites is expensive. It is often easier and cheaper to replace the satellites.

This artist's depiction shows what NASA's Restore-L system may look like in space.

But change might be coming. NASA and other groups are building robotic vehicles that can dock with old satellites and either repair or refuel them. One system, NASA's Restore-L, will refuel out-of-gas satellites, allowing them to continue operations. The vehicle will use robotic arms to carry out its job. NASA plans to launch Restore-L in 2019. Another idea is for robots to salvage parts from defunct satellites and use them to repair other broken satellites as they travel through space.

▶ SPACE-AGE GARBAGE TRUCKS

Donald Kessler warned that the amount of space junk is growing faster than the force of gravity is pulling junk back to the atmosphere. But what if we could fix the problem by pulling the junk down ourselves? Many space agencies and aerospace companies have drawn up plans to do just that. Engineers envision vehicles that will gather space junk and transfer it to the upper atmosphere, where it will rub against the air, grow hot, and burn up.

One proposed cleanup vehicle is called the TAMU Sweeper. Designed at Texas A&M University, this machine would use two long arms to snag space junk and fling it toward the atmosphere to burn up. The flinging motion would also propel the Sweeper through space. Another machine, the ElectroDynamic Debris Eliminator, designed by a company in South Carolina, would

A depiction of the proposed TAMU Sweeper traveling through space

An artist's drawing shows ESA's e.Deorbit (*left*) capturing space junk.

capture space junk in a giant net and tow it back to the atmosphere. Several space agencies also have cleanup vehicles on the drawing board. The European Space Agency wants to build a craft called e.Deorbit. It would capture space junk using robotic arms or nets and drag it back to the atmosphere. The Japanese Aerospace Exploration Agency is designing a tether that would use electricity to slow down space junk, causing it to fall into Earth's atmosphere to burn up. Researchers at NASA have proposed shooting down space junk with a giant laser aboard the ISS. Most of these ideas exist only on paper, however. They would be extremely expensive to build and operate and might never make it into space.

WHAT'S NEXT?

The space junk problem won't go away on its own. Space agencies, governments, and businesses all recognize the threat posed by pieces of metal and other debris speeding around the planet. A space junk strike on a satellite can disrupt communications and other systems on the ground. It might destroy a working space vehicle or even kill an astronaut. A new trend in space travel is space tourism. Private companies plan to take paying passengers on thrilling rides into Earth's atmosphere. But a space junk strike could spell disaster for a tourist vehicle.

Private companies such as SpaceX continue to build new spacecraft. As the number of spacecraft grows, so does the problem of garbage in space.

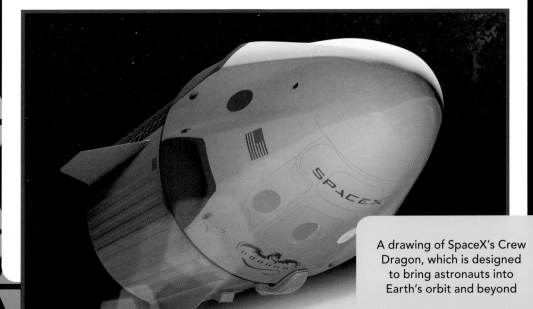

A drawing of SpaceX's Crew Dragon, which is designed to bring astronauts into Earth's orbit and beyond

US physicist and engineer Robert Hoyt is concerned about the growing problem of space junk.

Groups such as the Inter-Agency Space Debris Coordination Committee (IADC) have sounded the alarm about space junk. They have issued guidelines for satellite operators. For instance, the IADC requires operators to bring satellites back into the atmosphere within twenty-five years after their missions are over. But many satellite operators don't follow the guidelines.

Some experts say that pulling junk out of orbit is the only way to ensure safe satellite operations and space travel in the future. They say we must build space cleanup vehicles and put them to work. That will cost billions of dollars and require international cooperation. But experts say that the need is urgent. "A hundred

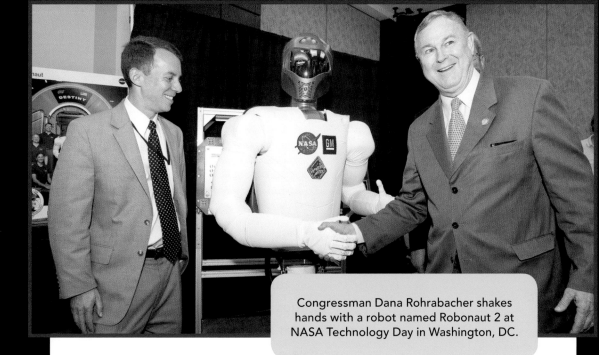

Congressman Dana Rohrabacher shakes hands with a robot named Robonaut 2 at NASA Technology Day in Washington, DC.

years from now, low earth orbit may be nearly unusable," warns US physicist and engineer Robert Hoyt. "Unless we go up and do active debris removal, then [the space junk problem] is going to get out of hand."

US representative Dana Rohrabacher of California echoed this warning at congressional hearings about space junk in 2014. He told his fellow lawmakers, "Debris is something that will limit humankind's ability to use space for our benefit. And we're getting to a point of saturation [levels of junk in space] now, where either we deal with it or we will suffer the consequences."

Source Notes

9   Jenna Iacurci, "Space Debris Could Create Real Life 'Gravity,' Lawmakers Say," *Nature World News*, May 10, 2014, http://www.natureworldnews.com/articles/6991/20140510/space-debris-could-create-real-life-gravity-lawmakers-say.htm.

21 Rosslyn Beeby, "Found in Space," *KnowHow Magazine*, September 2014, http://www.serc.org.au/wp-content/uploads/2014/07/Found-in-Space_KnowHow_Magazine.pdf.

43 Brian Bremner and Peter Robison, "Cleaning Up the Final Frontier," *Bloomberg*, January 16, 2014, http://www.bloomberg.com/news/articles/2014-01-16/space-junk-in-earth-orbit-the-cleanup-problem.

43 Ledyard King, "Space Junk a Growing Concern," *Asbury Park Press*, May 9, 2014, http://www.app.com/story/news/2014/05/09/space-junk-a-growing-concern/8919443.

Expand learning beyond the printed book. Download free, complementary educational resources for this book from our website, www.lerneresource.com.

Glossary

aerospace: the science dealing with Earth's atmosphere and the space around it

asteroid: a small rocky object orbiting the sun. Asteroids sometimes hit Earth's atmosphere.

astrophysicist: a scientist who studies space objects, particles, energy, and processes

atmosphere: a layer of gases surrounding a planet or another body in space

geostationary: a region of space more than 22,000 miles (35,406 km) above Earth.

gravity: a naturally occurring force that pulls objects in space toward one another

Kessler Syndrome: the process, first described by astrophysicist Donald Kessler, by which space junk hits other objects in space, breaks them apart, and creates even more space junk

laser: a device that produces powerful beams of light. Lasers can span Earth's orbit to find space junk.

meteor: a rocky or metallic object flying through space. Meteors sometimes hit Earth's atmosphere.

orbit: to travel around another object. For example, satellites orbit Earth. The path an object travels in space is also called its orbit.

radar: a system that emits radio waves. Engineers use radar to track objects in space.

satellite: a natural or human-made object that orbits another object in space. Human-made satellites do jobs such as monitoring weather on Earth, taking photographs, and sending communications signals.

SmallSat: a satellite that weighs less than 1,100 pounds (500 kg)

space junk: sometimes referred to as space debris, any human-made object traveling through space and not controlled by people on Earth

space walk: work done by astronauts outside their space vehicles

zombie satellite: a satellite that is out of operation and no longer in communication with controllers on Earth

Selected Bibliography

Bremner, Brian, and Peter Robison. "Cleaning Up the Final Frontier."
    Bloomberg, January 16, 2014. http://www.bloomberg.com/news
    /articles/2014-01-16/space-junk-in-earth-orbit-the-cleanup-problem.

Chang, Kenneth. "For Space Mess, Scientists Seek Celestial Broom." *New York
    Times*, February 18, 2012. http://www.nytimes.com/2012/02/19/science
    /space/for-space-mess-scientists-seek-celestial-broom.html.

Mann, Adam. "Space: The Final Frontier of Environmental Disasters?" *Wired*,
    July 15, 2013. http://www.wired.com/2013/07/space-environmentalism.

Stromberg, Joseph. "Space Garbage: The Dark Cloud Above." *Smithsonian.
    com*, January 26, 2012. http://www.smithsonianmag.com/science-nature
    /space-garbage-the-dark-cloud-above-80279582.

Further Reading and Websites

Silverman, Buffy. *Exploring Dangers in Space: Asteroids, Space Junk, and More.*
    Minneapolis: Lerner Publications, 2012.

———. *How Do Space Vehicles Work?* Minneapolis: Lerner Publications, 2013.

Space Junk Clean Up: 7 Wild Ways to Destroy Orbital Debris
    http://www.space.com/24895-space-junk-wild-clean-up-concepts.html

Space Junk Explained: How Orbital Debris Threatens Future of Spaceflight
    http://www.space.com/23039-space-junk-explained-orbital-debris
    -infographic.html

What Is Orbital Debris?
    http://www.nasa.gov/audience/forstudents/5-8/features/nasa-knows/what
    -is-orbital-debris-58.html

Young, Karen Romano. *Space Junk: The Dangers of Polluting Earth's Orbit.*
    Minneapolis: Twenty-First Century Books, 2016.

Index

Photo Acknowledgments

The images in this book are used with the permission of: NASA Orbital Debris Program Office, pp. 2, 7 (top), 8 (bottom), 10, 18, 20, 33, 34; © STR/AFP/Getty Images, p. 4; Britt Griswold/NASA Goddard Space Flight Center (CC BY 2.0), p. 5 (top); ESA, p. 5 (bottom); NASA, pp. 6, 9 (top), 11 (bottom), 13, 15, 22, 24, 25, 28, 29, 30, 37, 38; ESA-J.Mai, p. 7 (bottom); © IQOQI Vienna, Austrian Academy of Sciences, p. 8 (top); Izumi Hansen/NASA, p. 9 (bottom); Asif A. Siddiqi/NASA, p. 11 (top); ESA-P. Carril, p. 12; ESA-D. Ducros, p. 14; Everett Collection/Newscom, p. 16 (top); Mark Wolfe/FEMA, p. 16 (bottom); Photo courtesy of Nacogdoches Police, p. 17 (top); ESA–AOES-Medialab, p. 17 (bottom); © Rlandmann/Wikimedia Commons (CC BY-SA 3.0), p. 19 (top); James Blair/JSC/NASA, p. 19 (bottom); © Mitch Ames/Wikimedia Commons (CC BY-SA 4.0), p. 21; Bill Stafford/NASA, p. 23; US Air Force, p. 26; © DARPA/Wikimedia Commons, p. 27; © Lockheed Martin Corporation, p. 31; Arnold Engineering Development Complex/US Air Force, p. 32; ESA/Denmann Production, p. 35 (top); © Darren Whittingham/Shutterstock.com, p. 35 (bottom); NASA/NOAA GOES Project, p. 36; © Jonathan Missel/Texas A&M, p. 39; ESA/Mixed-Reality Communication GmbH, p. 40; © SpaceX, p. 41; © Signe Brewster, p. 42; Carla Cioffi/NASA, p. 43.

Front cover: ESA.